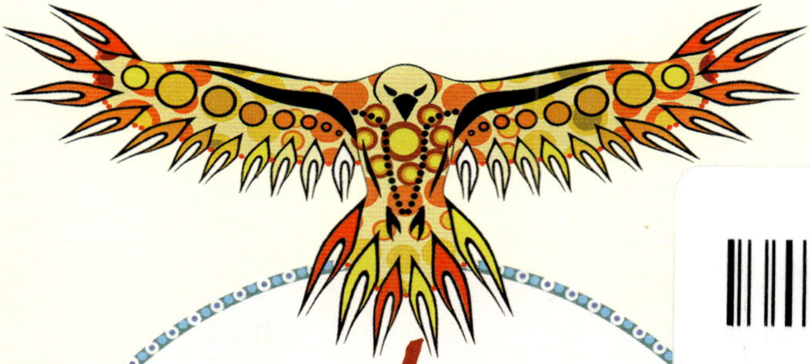

Firehawk

An Australian First Nations Tale

Retold by Gregg Dreise

Illustrated by Kristy Dreise

ISBN: 9781398377240

Text © Gregg Dreise
Illustrations, design and layout © 2023 Hodder & Stoughton Ltd
First published in 2023 by Hodder & Stoughton Limited
(for its Hodder Education imprint, part of the Hodder Education Group),
An Hachette UK Company
Carmelite House, 50 Victoria Embankment, London EC4Y 0DZ
www.hoddereducation.com

Impression number 10 9 8 7 6 5 4 3 2 1
Year 2027 2026 2025 2024 2023

Author: Gregg Dreise
Series Editor: Catherine Coe
Commissioning Editor: Hamish Baxter
Cover Illustrators: Gregg Dreise and Tika and Tata/Bright Group International
Internal Illustrator: Kristy Dreise
Educational Reviewer: Pauline Allen
Page design and layouts: Gary Kilpatrick
Editor: Amy Tyrer

With thanks to the schools that took part in the development of *Reading Planet* KS2, including: Ancaster CE Primary School, Ancaster; Downsway Primary School, Reading; Ferry Lane Primary School, London; Foxborough Primary School, Slough; Griffin Park Primary School, Blackburn; St Barnabas CE First & Middle School, Pershore; Tranmoor Primary School, Doncaster; and Wilton CE Primary School, Wilton.

All rights reserved. Apart from any use permitted under UK copyright law, no part of this publication may be reproduced or transmitted in any form or by any means, electronic or mechanical, including photocopying and recording, or held within any information storage and retrieval system, without permission in writing from the publisher or under licence from the Copyright Licensing Agency Limited. Further details of such licences (for reprographic reproduction) may be obtained from the Copyright Licensing Agency Limited, https://www.cla.co.uk/

A catalogue record for this title is available from the British Library.

Printed in India.

Orders: Please contact Hachette UK Distribution, Hely Hutchinson Centre, Milton Road, Didcot, Oxfordshire, OX11 7HH.
Telephone: (44) 01235 400555. Email: primary@hachette.co.uk.

Hachette UK's policy is to use papers that are natural, renewable and recyclable products and made from wood grown in well-managed forests and other controlled sources. The logging and manufacturing processes are expected to conform to the environmental regulations of the country of origin.

Contents

Chapter 1 4

Chapter 2 8

Chapter 3 14

Chapter 4 21

Chapter 5 28

Chapter 6 33

***Pronunciation guide**
Euahlayi: say *You-al-ee-eye*
Bayri: say *Bay-ree*
Garbayn: say *Gar-bain*
Biamme: say *Bye-aim-me*
Nginda gamil gidgay inye lap-lap:
  say *Nin-dah gah-mill gid-jar in-yee lap-lap*
Wii-Wandabah: say *We Wand-dar-bar*
Gali-Thawun: say *Gar-lee Thar-won*
Kene: say *Ken-ney*

Wantima: say *Want-tim-mah*
Nginda winunga: say *Nin-dah win-nung-ga*
Nginda yugaay: say *Nin-dah yug-gay*
Nginda ngumala: say *Nin-dah num-mah-lah*
Boreen: say *Bore-een*
Yulagee Bundar: say *You-lah-gee Bun-dar*

Chapter 1

The beginning of life in Australia was the Dreamtime. This was a time when the Earth was changing. A time when life as we know it today was being created. It was the time of Father Sky and Mother Earth coming together to create magic. The Ancestral Beings were creator spirits who used magic to shape hills and rivers. New creatures were emerging and beings changed into the characters that walk, fly and swim throughout Australia today.

Australia was – and still is – broken into over two hundred Countries. One of these Countries is Euahlayi*, the home of this story.

Two brothers lived in Euahlayi Country during the Dreamtime. Bayri* was a tall and proud hunter who always listened to his Elders and learned to respect Mother Earth and Father Sky. He listened to nature and followed the circles of life, to stay connected to Country and live off the land. The Elders were extremely proud of the wise, young man that Bayri had quickly become.

His little brother Garbayn* was different. He loved adventure. He struggled to gain the same respect in the community that his elder brother had earned. The wise Elders taught their community to be patient, but Garbayn was sadly impatient. The members of his community all knew that everyone was different. Differences were not seen as a bad thing. They all knew that everyone was good at something. Sometimes, it took a while longer for people to find the thing that they were good at. Garbayn just needed more time to show that he could be good at something.

Each time Bayri sat with Garbayn to pass on the wisdom of the Ancestors, his little brother's thoughts seemed to float like wispy clouds on the breeze. Garbayn was a daydreamer.

Each day, the two brothers hunted together. They talked about the knowledge and wisdom of Biamme* – the son of The Great One … the mighty spirit in the sky. Biamme was a magic man. The two brothers knew to follow his teachings and traditions. It was an honour for Garbayn to finally be initiated. This meant that he was now old enough to be able to go hunting with the men. Garbayn was proud of his initiation marks. His older brother Bayri loved seeing pride in his little brother. Bayri thought that this new-found pride would be the start of something special for his little brother. He knew that something special was coming for them both.

At the end of each day's hunt, Bayri would successfully provide food for his community to eat well, but Garbayn only seemed to be able to provide laughter.

"When are you going to teach me how to hunt with fire?" Garbayn asked his older brother.

"You are not ready. And neither is Mother Earth," Bayri replied. *"Nginda gamil gidgay inye lap-lap** – perhaps when you stop having ants in your pants." But the ants were always in Garbayn's pants – he could never sit still.

In time, Garbayn finally improved his hunting effort and skills, and began to provide food for his community. In time, he began to show more maturity for sitting and listening.

One day, Bayri simply stated, "Mother Earth is ready for me to teach you about *Wii-Wandabah** – Fire-Spirit."

"Why does Mother Earth decide the right time and not you?" Garbayn asked.

Bayri loved seeing his younger brother beginning to ask sensible questions.

Bayri proudly answered, "Because when we begin to wake up with *Gali-Thawun** – dew on the grass – it is time for teenagers to learn about fire. It is a safe time. The cold morning dew stops fire from spreading uncontrollably."

Chapter 2

Garbayn was full of excitement as his elder brother began to teach him about fire. Bayri took out his fire sticks from where they were hidden in the highest part of the rock shelter. He explained how they were kept up there to remain dry. He explained that he wrapped the fire sticks in kangaroo leather to keep them dry. He told his little brother how the ends were always kept in the bark pouch, wrapped in string covered in beeswax mixed with tree sap. The more Bayri explained, the more the ants began to return to Garbayn's pants.

"When am I going to start a fire?" he nagged.

"We are not at that part yet – be patient."

But Garbayn was impatient.

Fire sticks are made from *Kene**
– grass tree stems. You need two sticks to make fire sticks. The thicker one becomes the base that lies on the ground.

Bayri demonstrated how to make a saddle on the base stick.

He used a rock to make a resting place in the base stick for the top rubbing stick. He showed Garbayn how to prepare both sticks so that they would work together smoothly.

"When am I going to start a fire?" Garbayn repeated.

"We are not at that part yet – be—"

"Yeah, yeah! Be patient!" Garbayn interrupted, mimicking his brother.

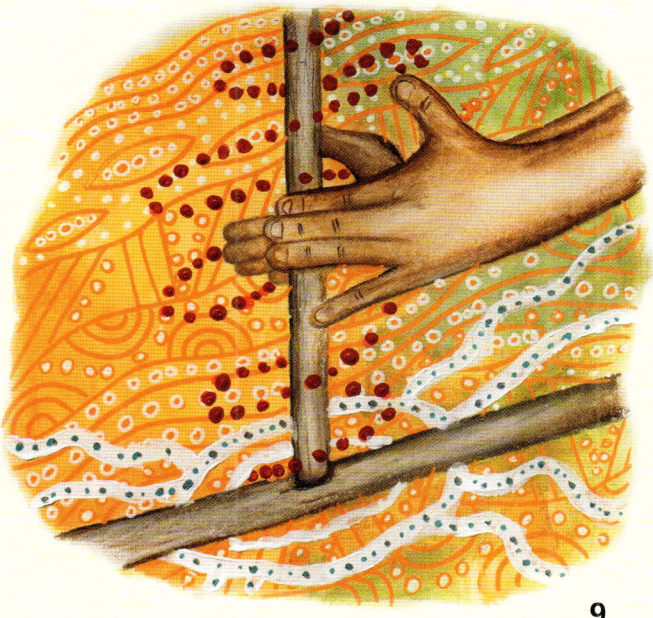

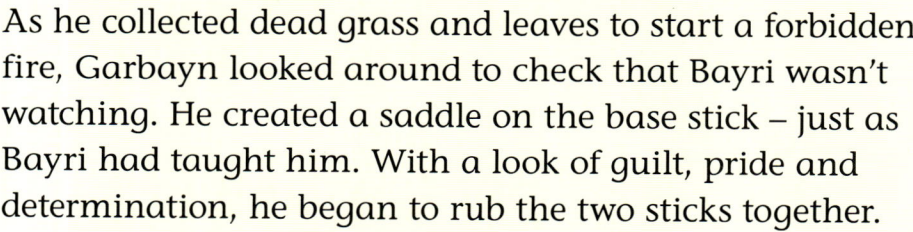

Eventually, the ants in Garbayn's pants grew too bothersome and he had to go off on a frustrated walk. He needed some time to cool down, before he got in trouble … yet again.

On this walk, he saw two perfectly straight sticks lying on the ground. They looked like great fire sticks to Garbayn. He knew that he was meant to wait, but he couldn't stop himself.

As he collected dead grass and leaves to start a forbidden fire, Garbayn looked around to check that Bayri wasn't watching. He created a saddle on the base stick – just as Bayri had taught him. With a look of guilt, pride and determination, he began to rub the two sticks together.

Garbayn rubbed frantically and happily. He knew that starting a fire took his brother about a minute. He rubbed swiftly and determinedly. He knew that it was taking longer than his brother. He rubbed madly and feverishly. He knew that he didn't like the pain in his now-hot hands and the throb in his arms. He knew that he wanted to give up … But he knew that he also didn't want to give up. The pain was now burying deeper into his hands and arms. In an explosion of frustration, he gave up and threw the sticks over towards the tall rocks.

As Garbayn flopped down in a frustrated heap, he thought about his brother and the Elders. He knew that they would think, *Typical Garbayn ... he can't do anything right.* This thought gave him a new boost of determination. *What would my brother say?* He asked himself. *He would use an encouraging word like* Wantima* – *yeah,* Wantima *... It means no one cares about the best ... your best is all that matters.* Wantima – *rise up to your best.*

With those words of encouragement, he rose up and marched over to regather the two sticks that he had just thrown away. He sat back down over the bed of dead grass and kept trying.

Garbayn continued stubbornly all afternoon.

Although to regather when one of his now-many blisters finally popped, he gave up again.

Garbayn was flabbergasted to hear his elder brother's voice from above.

"Now that you have finally given up, come and learn all of the things that you did wrong – but only after your wounds have healed. Clay from the healing pools will help your hands."

Bayri then glided down from the tree branch behind Garbayn.

Garbayn couldn't believe that his older brother had been watching him. He wanted to be mad, but he knew that his kind-hearted brother would fix his aching hands and still be patient enough to teach him. He was disappointed in his own failure, yet proud of his older brother, Bayri.

Chapter 3

Two weeks went by. Two long weeks of waiting. Garbayn's blisters finally healed. With this, he sulked back to his big brother Bayri and found the word that he always struggled with: "Sorry." He then sat in silence with his chin sinking into his chest. He listened to all of the reasons why young ones need to look, listen and learn.

"Nginda winunga* – you listen. Nginda yugaay* – you look. Nginda ngumala* – you learn," Bayri told him sternly. "When you learn, you will know that you actually did lots of things right. But you must be patient. You need to follow the teachings of Biamme. You must use the right sticks."

"What? What do you mean 'the right sticks'?" asked the surprised Garbayn.

"Did you think that fire sticks could be made out of any wood?" replied Bayri.

"Well … um … yes," Garbayn stammered.

Bayri kept his wonderful patience and wisdom as he explained, "Remember, fire sticks can only be made from *Kene* – grass tree stems. Today, I will show you where to get these … but you have to promise to be responsible – otherwise you will have to wait until next year."

"I promise," replied Garbayn with that big smile.

As they walked on Country, Garbayn remained silent. Bayri taught without interruption that whole day.

Bayri reminded Garbayn, "*Kene* need to remain dry, and they must only be used when supervised by an Elder."

Garbayn agreed as he was trying to contain his excitement – but these last rules stuck in his head …

"If you don't follow these rules for the next year, you will be banned from fire sticks for two years – plus you will receive the harsh punishment of *Boreen*."

Garbayn did not want to be in the middle of a ring of Elders with spears. He knew that *Boreen* meant that he could be hurt, so he agreed.

Finally, Garbayn *learnt* from his elder brother. Finally, Garbayn could start a fire from rubbing two sticks together … the right type of sticks. It took a lot of time and effort.

It took a lot of aches from little muscles he didn't really know that he had. But it was worth the effort ... he loved being able to create fire with his bare hands and two sticks.

Garbayn thought it was finally time to go hunting, but as was tradition, they had to participate in the hunting dance first. Garbayn loved this dance; it was both a dance to teach techniques, plus a traditional childhood game. It was a game where young children got the chance to pretend that they were adult hunters.

The two brothers organised a traditional hunting dance to celebrate that Garbayn would go and hunt kangaroos the next day.

That night, after dinner, the corroboree dance was performed with all of the young boys and girls. It was called *Yulagee Bundar**, which means 'Copy Kangaroos', and was both Garbayn and Bayri's favourite dance.

The community sat around the outside of the dance circle of sand by the river. The sight of the firelight shimmering under the moon was unforgettable. The sound of the didgeridoo, clapsticks and choir of harmonies was unforgettable. The smiles of the whole community watching on were unforgettable. The pride of the two brothers leading the young ones of their community was truly unforgettable.

Everyone slept well under the glorious stars that night.

At first light, Bayri woke Garbayn up. For the first time in Garbayn's life, he was excited to get up at the crack of dawn. Finally, he was going fire stick hunting with Bayri.

Without any words, Bayri showed him where the kangaroos were grazing. In a whisper, Bayri taught him which way the wind was blowing and how the wind spirit created the direction of travel for fires. Bayri whispered to him the last reminders before starting the fire. Bayri explained that everything they were going to do was in order to control the fire that they were about to create.

Bayri truly was a very patient and caring teacher.

Bayri showed Garbayn where he would hide beyond the creek. He showed Garbayn how his fire would chase the kangaroos straight to his elder brother – who could hunt one of them.

"The kangaroos will only be concerned about the fire – they will not have eyes for any hunters," Bayri taught.

For the first time ever, Garbayn started a fire that was to ambush kangaroos. He was finally a part of what he had always dreamed about – fire stick hunting.

Bayri disappeared into bushland beyond the creek. Garbayn had the fire going in around a minute. His smile stretched like a dazzling rainbow across Father Sky. The wind pushed his fire straight to the creek … just as Bayri had planned. He knew that once it made it to the creek bed, the fire would go out and everyone would be safe.

Everything worked exactly as Bayri planned. The fire chased the kangaroos to the creek. Bayri successfully speared a kangaroo that was only concerned about the fire.

That night, everyone celebrated the success of the fire stick hunt. The smell of the food danced through the air. The taste of the kangaroo meat, vegetables and damper* danced around the happy people's mouths. The sound of the music danced around the joyful dance circle. The sound of laughter danced around their home. The family pride danced around their happy hearts. Garbayn was the proudest he had ever been. That night, the twinkle of the stars danced around Garbayn as he fell asleep knowing that he finally had two of the most beautiful things in life that he had always yearned for: love and respect.

*damper is a traditional aboriginal bread

Chapter 4

The next day, Bayri took Garbayn to check that the smouldering heat from yesterday's fire could not start again. He showed his little brother how to check that everything that they had created was safe for their community. They were both pleased to see that the morning dew had sucked the last life from the fire … just as Biamme had taught them.

"That's why we wait for Mother Earth to tell us when we can do this. If you do this in the hot, windy months, that fire could never be controlled."

Bayri looked at Garbayn to make sure that he was listening. He was proud of how his little brother had grown up lately.

"Look how low that fire was," he stated as he pointed to the minimal damage on the trees. "Big bushfires get out of control – they go to the top of trees, killing all of the animals trying to get away from the flames. Just like that koala up there. He is safe." Bayri was proud of his knowledge and understanding of his Country.

Garbayn looked up, amazed. He hadn't even seen the koala up in the tree.

"Big bushfires can turn wombats' burrows into a ground oven. It gets too hot for that little fella in there – so hot that burrowing animals die," Bayri explained wisely.

Garbayn looked down surprised. He hadn't even seen this wombat's burrow down in the ground.

"And see these seeds here?" continued Bayri, "These seeds will now open up with the heat to begin new life – only fire can open these seeds."

Two weeks after the fire, Bayri took Garbayn back to their fire stick hunting location. The once-blackened burned patch was now sprouting with new, fresh, green grass shoots. The animals were all returning to that area to munch on the fresh, new, juicy, green grass. By now, Bayri and Garbayn were fire stick hunting successfully in new areas each week.

They only had to do it once per week to feed their clan group. Everyone knew not to hunt large animals too much, as the plants and smaller animals provided them with all of the food that they needed. Everyone was always taught by Biamme to only take what you need – never be greedy.

After the season of spring began to move into the blaze of summer, Bayri informed Garbayn that their fire stick hunting had now come to an end.

"What? No way! It works so well – we need to keep doing it!" urged Garbayn.

"No – Mother Earth doesn't allow that – it is now too dangerous. The wind and the heat can make fires out of control," Bayri replied.

Garbayn was not happy that he could no longer go fire stick hunting.

"Are you saying that we have to go back to the hard work of tracking animals and throwing spears and boomerangs?" asked a gloomy Garbayn.

"Yes. It is the way of our people," Bayri replied as he continued through the bush, looking for ideas for their next meal.

As the heat in Euahlayi Country began to soar, the hunting of large animals faded. Hunters unsuccessfully followed animal footprints for days. The longer-range throws of spears and boomerangs made hunting more challenging. Garbayn had returned to being a not very successful hunter. His head now sank low like each setting sun. His silly behaviour now returned like a boomerang.

All he wanted to do was fire stick hunt. These thoughts stayed with him during months of disappointment.

Garbayn had finally had enough.

"I know how to do it. I am going to fire stick hunt – it works," he muttered to himself.

He saw a mob of kangaroos grazing, but they were too fast for him to even get close.

Just as his brother had shown him, he checked the wind and the creek position to start the fire.

He crept to the high rocky shelters and fetched his fire sticks.

Chapter 5

As Garbayn returned to the mob of kangaroos, he knew that it would be easier to hunt with fire. Only this time he had to work without his brother. Even so, it would still be easier than all of that tracking.

"Let the kangaroos come to me," he told himself. "It doesn't matter that I don't have my brother … I have speed on my side."

With that, he rubbed his fire sticks together and started a grass fire. He knew that once the fire got going, he had to run around the kangaroos. He told himself that he was fast enough to get around to the other side of the creek and surprise them.

With a huge grin of excitement, Garbayn started his first fire in months. He loved seeing his smoke turn into a fire. The familiar crackle soon alerted the kangaroos. As he ran around the kangaroos to get to the other side of the creek, he saw the kangaroos' ears turning … they knew that they were in danger.

By the time he got to the creek, he saw that the fire was too fast for him. So were the kangaroos.

To his surprise, that small fire had soon grown bigger with the wind. It was now big enough to jump the little creek, and it continued to grow into a big bushfire. Trouble was raging all around Garbayn.

As Garbayn feared for his life, he began to try to outrun the fire. But the fire was catching him as he ran towards the homes of his community.

Luckily for Garbayn, a gift from Father Sky came in the form of a rain cloud. Light rain quickly developed into a drenching downpour that put the trouble out. The fire was gone.

When the Elders arrived with Bayri to see what was going on, Garbayn lied.

"A big bolt of lightning crashed down from that angry cloud – it obviously started this fire."

The Elders agreed that it was lucky that the rain cloud was there, otherwise the people and animals of their community would have been in great trouble.

A month passed, and Garbayn longed for the return of fire stick hunting. The urge grew from a spark into an internal blaze … he knew that he had to try again. He told himself that he had learned from his last mistake.

This time, he was going to run with the fire, instead of going around it. This time, he would send the fire to the lake, because he knew that no fire could jump that. This time, he planned to follow the kangaroos instead of going around them, as his brother had taught him. He planned to get one of the kangaroos as it tried to find shelter in the lake. Obviously, the kangaroos would be looking at the fire – not him.

"I am brilliant." Garbayn smiled to himself. "The first wise hunter to work out how to fire stick hunt solo."

This time, he set the fire, as planned. He ran straight towards the kangaroos, as planned. The kangaroos had nowhere to go but into the safety of the lake. But, unfortunately, that was the only part of the plan that worked.

Before Garbayn knew it, that inferno was raging around him from every direction. He was now in the middle of an uncontrolled fire …

"Help!" Garbayn screamed from the top of his lungs. "Bayri! Help!" he screeched.

Chapter 6

The fire raced around him, sending fear to his heart. The fire flashed around him at the same time as his brother's words of wisdom – the words that he had foolishly ignored. The sound of flames shrieked around Garbayn, mirroring his own cries for his brother's help. The flames screamed around his memories of growing up near this lake. He couldn't see how he could possibly get out of these walls of fire that surrounded him.

His cries for help struggled to compete against the roar of the flames.

From the rocky ridges above, Bayri heard the screams for help from his little brother. He ran with greater speed and determination than he had ever run throughout his whole life.

From a high rocky ledge, he looked down to see his little brother surrounded by a furious fire beside the lake. Bayri was normally quick to work out a plan, but his brain left him with no logical way to get to his brother in time. The only way he could think of to get out of this situation was with magic. The only person he knew that could create magic was Biamme.

"Help!" Bayri sang from the top of his lungs. "Help me, Biamme!"

Luckily for the two brothers, Biamme appeared beside Bayri.

"Biamme – save him! I will do anything to save my little brother – please – anything!" Bayri begged.

Biamme blew with all of his might, but even his magic was not strong enough to put out the fire. He held the walls of flames back from Garbayn, but could not extinguish them.

"I will stay here and keep the flames off your little brother for as long as I can, but I have to send you above him to save him," Biamme explained in between his strong wind blasts.

"I will do anything to save my little brother – anything!" Bayri pleaded, looking up to the tall, strong Biamme.

Knowing that time was running out, Biamme pulled his magic stone out of his snake-skin belt and pointed it at Bayri. Bayri was surrounded by a blast of energy.

With this powerful burst of energy, Biamme began his magic song. As the song echoed around the rocky outcrop, so too did the wind …

The song in the wind from the magic stone spun around Bayri. The wind from Biamme's mouth continued to blast across to protect Garbayn from the wall of flames that surrounded him.

The magic energy from Biamme's stone turned into a dazzling display of light and sound. The magic of the energy from Biamme's breath began to fade. For the first time in his life, Biamme felt weak. His cold blast of protection towards the little brother in the fire began to fade. The wind was now no longer strong enough to hold back the fire from Garbayn.

The wind and energy from the magic stone began to fade, but thankfully Biamme's magic had worked. As Biamme collapsed on to the rock, Bayri was transformed into a rain cloud. That rain cloud quickly pushed out over his little brother. Water raced out of the magic cloud made by big brother Bayri's tears.

Bayri was now a rain cloud spirit. His magic tears showered his little brother to save his life. Garbayn, the little brother, was saved. Now rising above the fire, Biamme magically turned that little brother into a bird.

That bird looked brown, black and almost burning as he flew from the dangerous, big bushfire.

The spirits of the two brothers were now forever changed into something else … something special.

Today, those birds are called *Wii-Garbayn* – firehawks. They contain the spirit of the little brother from the Dreamtime – Garbayn.

Since the day of that bushfire, rainwater falling from the sky is called *Bayri-Gali*. It contains the spirit of the elder brother, Bayri, from back in the Dreamtime.

This story is retold to continue spreading the wisdom of the Ancestors. It is used to pass on the when and where of fire stick hunting and the importance of back-burning. This burning is a traditional practice that Aboriginal Australians have always done to protect the land from destructive out-of-control fires by using regular, small, controlled fires.

This story reminds us of how essential water is – of Bayri's spirit.

Today, firehawks still use fire to hunt. If you watch carefully during Australian bushfires, firehawk birds swoop down and capture sticks that are on fire. They swiftly drop the sticks over burrows of animals that they have been trying to hunt. The fire then chases the little animals out of their hiding places, so that the firehawks can swoop down and catch their prey.

The Elders see this amazing bird use fire for their hunt, and they pass down the wisdom of the Ancestors to show the next generation how to respect and use fire.

Our Elders tell this story to the next generations to remind us of the spirit and love of these two brothers from the Dreamtime. This story is shared to remind us to stay connected to Country and to understand that everyone is different. This story is shared to remind us to shower our friends and family with guidance, wisdom, patience, protection and love for one another. Just as Bayri would do for his little brother Garbayn.

Now answer the questions …

1. Where did Bayri and Garbayn live?

2. '"Yeah, yeah! Be patient!" Garbayn interrupted, mimicking his brother.' (page 10) What does 'mimicking' mean?

3. Why did Garbayn think it was finally time to go hunting (page 16)?

4. What happened when Garbayn first went fire stick hunting by himself in Chapter 5?

5. What did you think would happen when Garbayn decided to try again to go fire stick hunting by himself?

6. Why did Garbayn think of his memories of growing up near the lake when he was surrounded by flames (page 33)?

7. The author uses repetition regularly in the story, such as the repetition of 'This story' on page 39. How does this add to the meaning?

8. What would you have done if you were Garbayn's older brother? Would you have been so patient with him?